Hillstrom's Rebuild

A Framework for Leaders Tasked with Fixing a Business

Kevin Hillstrom

Acknowledgements

A shout-out to my wife, who sat patiently and waited for me to finish typing more than 9,000 words so that we can have fun together!

13 Digit ISBN: 978-1539320340

Published in the United States of America by Kevin Hillstrom

Available from Amazon.com and other retailers.

Manufactured in the United States of America
First Edition

Cover Design: Kevin Hillstrom and Createspace.com
Cover Art: Kevin Hillstrom

Table of Contents

A Framework for Measuring Wins and Losses   7

What Went Wrong?   27

Setting Up a Winning Plan   40

Setting Objectives   47

Encouragement   52

A Framework for Measuring Wins and Losses

In sports, it is easy to tell when a team is not performing well. Just look at the standings! For instance, my Green Bay Packers have had ups and downs, but for the most part, they have enjoyed a twenty-five year run of excellent performance. Look at the record below, what do you observe?

1991 = 4 wins, 12 losses. Coach fired.

1992 = 9 wins, 7 losses.

1993 = 9 wins, 7 losses. Lost in Divisional Round of Playoffs.

1994 = 9 wins, 7 losses. Lost in Divisional Round of Playoffs.

1995 = 11 wins, 5 losses. Lost in NFC Championship Game.

1996 = 13 wins, 3 losses. Won Super Bowl!!

1997 = 13 wins, 3 losses. Lost Super Bowl.

1998 = 11 wins, 5 losses. Lost in Wild Card Round. Coach Resigned.

1999 = 8 wins, 8 losses. Coach Fired.

2000 = 9 wins, 7 losses.

2001 = 12 wins, 4 losses. Lost in Divisional Round of Playoffs.

2002 = 12 wins, 4 losses. Lost in Wild Card Round of Playoffs.

2003 = 10 wins, 6 losses. Lost in Divisional Round of Playoffs.

2004 = 10 wins, 6 losses. Lost in Wild Card Round of Playoffs.

2005 = 4 wins, 12 losses. Coach Fired.

2006 = 8 wins, 8 losses.

2007 = 13 wins, 3 losses. Lost in NFC Championship Game.

2008 = 6 wins, 10 losses.

2009 = 11 wins, 5 losses. Lost in Wild Card Round of Playoffs.

2010 = 10 wins, 6 losses. Won Super Bowl!!

2011 = 15 wins, 1 loss. Lost in Divisional Round of Playoffs.

2012 = 11 wins, 5 losses. Lost in Divisional Round of Playoffs.

2013 = 8 wins, 7 losses, 1 tie. Lost in Wild Card Round of Playoffs.

2014 = 12 wins, 4 losses. Lost in NFC Championship Game.

2015 = 10 wins, 6 losses. Lost in Divisional Round of Playoffs.

It's not hard to see the ups and downs, is it? Wins are depicted graphically below:

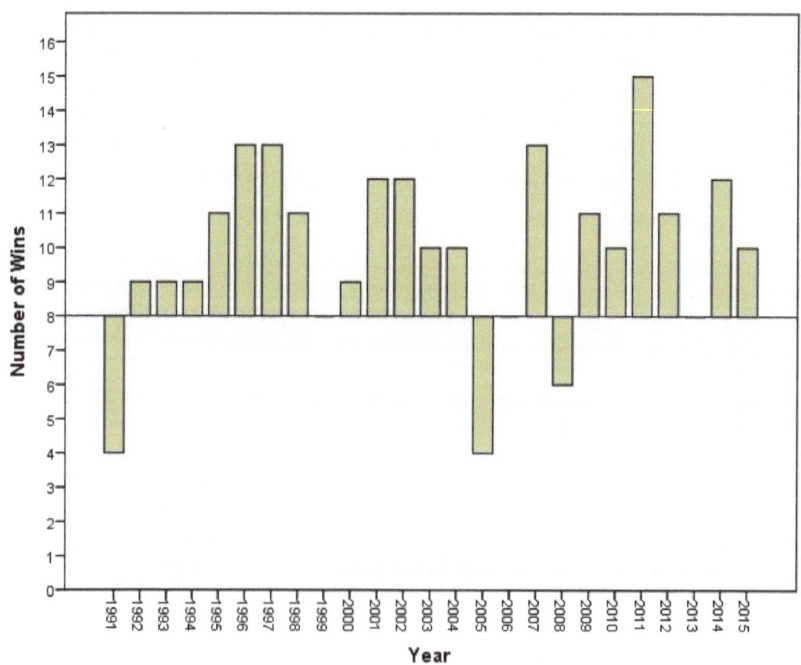

The team built a "winner" … slowly improving from 1992 – 1994. From 1995 – 1998, the team performed at a high level. Then we observe a "rebuilding project" from 1999 – 2000. Green Bay did not make the playoffs. From 2001 – 2004, the team was good, but not great. In 2005, the team only won four games, and embarked on another rebuilding project. Results from 2005 – 2008 were "spotty", with a breakout year in 2007. In 2009, the team began to perform at a high level once again, winning a Super Bowl in 2010 and achieving a franchise-high fifteen wins in 2011.

Notice that the rebuilding projects (for the most part) did not result in a prolonged stretch of bad seasons.

Speaking of bad seasons, some teams seem to always be in rebuilding mode. Take the Detroit Lions, for instance. They have not been able to sustain success in the past twenty-five years.

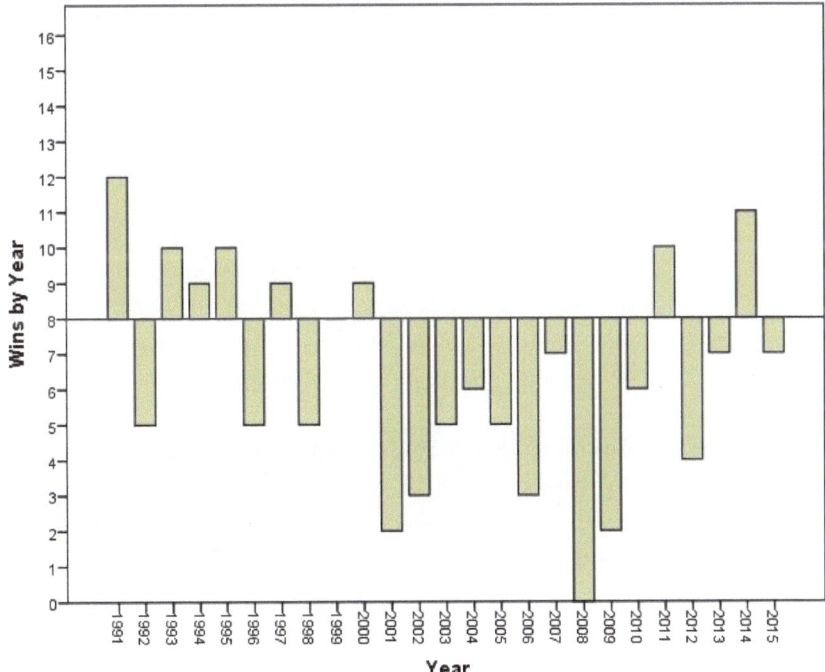

In sports, we can easily measure when a team is performing well, and we can easily measure when a team is struggling. It isn't much different in business, my friends. Especially with publicly traded companies. Take a look at the table below. The table represents annual net sales, gross margin data, and profit data for Chico's (taken from their 10-K annual statements, numbers in thousands).

Year	Net Sales	Gross Mrg	Pre-Tax $	Margin %	PreTax %
2001	$259,446	$150,775	$45,772	58.1%	17.6%
2002	$378,085	$224,148	$68,043	59.3%	18.0%
2003	$531,108	$321,338	$107,676	60.5%	20.3%
2004	$768,499	$471,022	$161,662	61.3%	21.0%
2005	$1,066,882	$654,974	$226,703	61.4%	21.2%
2006	$1,640,927	$967,185	$166,636	58.9%	10.2%
2007	$1,714,326	$969,061	$88,875	56.5%	5.2%
2008	$1,582,405	$819,492	($19,137)	51.8%	-1.2%
2009	$1,713,150	$959,741	$69,646	56.0%	4.1%
2010	$1,904,954	$1,068,575	$115,394	56.1%	6.1%
2011	$2,196,360	$1,226,371	$140,874	55.8%	6.4%
2012	$2,581,057	$1,451,800	$180,219	56.2%	7.0%
2013	$2,586,037	$1,416,631	$65,883	54.8%	2.5%
2014	$2,675,211	$1,426,322	$64,641	53.3%	2.4%
2015	$2,642,309	$1,430,757	$1,946	54.1%	0.1%

Chico's sells Women's Apparel. Sales grew through 2012, as the brand was able to expand the store portfolio from 250 stores in 2001 to 1,357 stores in 2012.

Look at the Pre-Tax Profit column (labeled Pre-Tax $). What do you see when you observe this metric? This metric looks a lot like the won-lost record of a sports team, doesn't it? Profit peaked in 2005, followed by a loss in 2008. Then the business was rebuilt, with profit peaking in 2012. Since 2012, sales have not grown, and profit continually declined.

Look at the Pre-Tax Profit Percentage column (labeled PreTax%). Here, we divide pre-tax profit by net sales, allowing us to measure the quality of profit. One might say that through 2005, Chico's was a "Championship" level brand. It's hard to generate more than 10% pre-tax profit in any given year, much less six-straight years (from 2001 – 2006). But since then, Chico's has been exceptionally average. Rebuilding efforts that began in 2009 yield reasonable performance through 2012. Since the end of 2012, Chico's is not performing well, and is in need of being rebuilt once again.

Here is a similar table for Macy's (all subsequent financial data obtained from company 10-K annual statements).

Year	Net Sales	Pre-Tax $	PreTax %
2001	$15,785,000	$764,000	4.8%
2002	$15,571,000	$1,048,000	6.7%
2003	$15,412,000	$1,084,000	7.0%
2004	$15,776,000	$1,116,000	7.1%
2005	$22,390,000	$2,044,000	9.1%
2006	$26,970,000	$1,446,000	5.4%
2007	$26,313,000	$1,320,000	5.0%
2008	$24,892,000	($4,938,000)	-19.8%
2009	$23,489,000	$507,000	2.2%
2010	$25,003,000	$1,320,000	5.3%
2011	$26,405,000	$1,968,000	7.5%
2012	$27,686,000	$2,102,000	7.6%
2013	$27,931,000	$2,290,000	8.2%
2014	$28,105,000	$2,390,000	8.5%
2015	$27,079,000	$1,678,000	6.2%

What do you observe (Net Sales and Profit figures in thousands, FYI)?

We observe that the business peaked in 2005, generating significant growth, a near doubling of pre-tax profit, and a 9.1% pre-tax profit rate. This business was very healthy in 2005.

Business bottomed-out in 2008, with a whopping loss of nearly five billion dollars. The rebuild began in 2009, as Macy's generated profit once again. By 2013 – 2014, the "omnichannel" approach to business worked for Macy's. Although growth was generally tepid, pre-tax profit surged over eight percent for two-consecutive years.

By 2015, sales were in decline and pre-tax profit suffered. In 2016, Macy's decided to replace their Chief Executive Officer.

Now compare Macy's to Nordstrom. The two companies technically "compete" against each other. How do the financials look?

Year	Net Sales	Pre-Tax $	PreTax %
2001	$5,607,687	$204,488	3.6%
2002	$5,944,656	$195,624	3.3%
2003	$6,448,678	$398,141	6.2%
2004	$7,131,388	$647,281	9.1%
2005	$7,722,860	$885,225	11.5%
2006	$8,561,000	$1,149,000	13.4%
2007	$8,828,000	$1,247,000	14.1%
2008	$8,272,000	$779,000	9.4%
2009	$8,258,000	$834,000	10.1%
2010	$9,310,000	$1,118,000	12.0%
2011	$10,497,000	$1,249,000	11.9%
2012	$11,762,000	$1,345,000	11.4%
2013	$12,166,000	$1,350,000	11.1%
2014	$13,110,000	$1,323,000	10.1%
2015	$14,095,000	$1,101,000	7.8%

The financial story is different at Nordstrom, isn't it? Pre-tax profit percentage follows a similar curve to Macy's. However, the quality of sales increases, pre-tax profit increase, and pre-tax profit rate is simply much higher than at Macy's. Notice that when the business bottomed-out in 2008, Nordstrom still generated $779,000,000 in pre-tax profit, and generated a 9.4% pre-tax profit rate. At the bottom of The Great Recession, Nordstrom produced quality-of-profit numbers that exceeded the rate Macy's generated in their best years.

In other words, Nordstrom exhibits performance similar to the Green Bay Packers. Macy's, however, exhibits performance directionally similar to the Detroit Lions.

But not all is good at Nordstrom.

Look at 2006. Nordstrom generated $8.6 billion in net sales, and $1.1 billion in pre-tax profit.

Look at 2015. Nordstrom generated $14.1 billion in net sales, and $1.1 billion in pre-tax profit.

In other words, Nordstrom increased sales by $5.5 billion in nine years, and the sales increase did not earn Nordstrom a single penny in pre-tax profit. Nordstrom is growing for the sake of growth, and cannot find a way to translate growth into profit. Nordstrom is not unlike a football team that can score 35 points per game, but has a defense that also gives up 35 points per game. Nordstrom is, in many ways, treading water. That being said, I'd rather be Nordstrom than Macy's, wouldn't you?

Here's a way to think of Chico's, Macy's, and Nordstrom. We could view each business as an NFL Franchise. We could use an equation to convert Sales Growth and Profit Quality into an NFL won-lost record. This methodology allows us to measure the quality of each year at Chico's, Macy's, and Nordstrom. In theory, we can measure the quality of your business as well!

For each of the three companies, I graded each year with a number of "wins", to parallel what an NFL team might experience.

Here's what the table looks like for Chico's.

Chicos Year	Net Sales	Pre-Tax $	PreTax %	N/S Growth	Profit Rate	Wins
2001	$259,446	$45,772	17.6%			
2002	$378,085	$68,043	18.0%	0.457	0.180	15
2003	$531,108	$107,676	20.3%	0.405	0.203	15
2004	$768,499	$161,662	21.0%	0.447	0.210	15
2005	$1,066,882	$226,703	21.2%	0.388	0.212	15
2006	$1,640,927	$166,636	10.2%	0.538	0.102	13
2007	$1,714,326	$88,875	5.2%	0.045	0.052	8
2008	$1,582,405	($19,137)	-1.2%	-0.077	-0.012	4
2009	$1,713,150	$69,646	4.1%	0.083	0.041	7
2010	$1,904,954	$115,394	6.1%	0.112	0.061	8
2011	$2,196,360	$140,874	6.4%	0.153	0.064	9
2012	$2,581,057	$180,219	7.0%	0.175	0.070	9
2013	$2,586,037	$65,883	2.5%	0.002	0.025	5
2014	$2,675,211	$64,641	2.4%	0.034	0.024	6
2015	$2,642,309	$1,946	0.1%	-0.012	0.001	4

This is the table for Macy's.

Macy's

Year	Net Sales	Pre-Tax $	PreTax %	N/S Growth	Profit Rate	Wins
2001	$15,785,000	$764,000	4.8%			
2002	$15,571,000	$1,048,000	6.7%	-0.014	0.067	6
2003	$15,412,000	$1,084,000	7.0%	-0.010	0.070	7
2004	$15,776,000	$1,116,000	7.1%	0.024	0.071	8
2005	$22,390,000	$2,044,000	9.1%	0.419	0.091	14
2006	$26,970,000	$1,446,000	5.4%	0.205	0.054	9
2007	$26,313,000	$1,320,000	5.0%	-0.024	0.050	5
2008	$24,892,000	($4,938,000)	-19.8%	-0.054	-0.198	2
2009	$23,489,000	$507,000	2.2%	-0.056	0.022	4
2010	$25,003,000	$1,320,000	5.3%	0.064	0.053	7
2011	$26,405,000	$1,968,000	7.5%	0.056	0.075	8
2012	$27,686,000	$2,102,000	7.6%	0.049	0.076	8
2013	$27,931,000	$2,290,000	8.2%	0.009	0.082	9
2014	$28,105,000	$2,390,000	8.5%	0.006	0.085	9
2015	$27,079,000	$1,678,000	6.2%	-0.037	0.062	6

And this is the table I created for Nordstrom.

Nordstrom

Year	Net Sales	Pre-Tax $	PreTax %	N/S Growth	Profit Rate	Wins
2001	$5,607,687	$204,488	3.6%			
2002	$5,944,656	$195,624	3.3%	0.060	0.033	8
2003	$6,448,678	$398,141	6.2%	0.085	0.062	9
2004	$7,131,388	$647,281	9.1%	0.106	0.091	12
2005	$7,722,860	$885,225	11.5%	0.083	0.115	12
2006	$8,561,000	$1,149,000	13.4%	0.109	0.134	14
2007	$8,828,000	$1,247,000	14.1%	0.031	0.141	11
2008	$8,272,000	$779,000	9.4%	-0.063	0.094	5
2009	$8,258,000	$834,000	10.1%	-0.002	0.101	6
2010	$9,310,000	$1,118,000	12.0%	0.127	0.120	13
2011	$10,497,000	$1,249,000	11.9%	0.127	0.119	13
2012	$11,762,000	$1,345,000	11.4%	0.121	0.114	13
2013	$12,166,000	$1,350,000	11.1%	0.034	0.111	11
2014	$13,110,000	$1,323,000	10.1%	0.078	0.101	12
2015	$14,095,000	$1,101,000	7.8%	0.075	0.078	10

Next, I divided wins by 16, to represent the winning percentage through an entire season. Finally, I created a Logistic Regression equation to assign a Winning Percentage to each year, based on Net Sales Growth and Pre-Tax Profit Rate. Here is the fitted equation.

Variables in the Equation

		B	S.E.	Wald	df	Sig.	Exp(B)
Step 1[a]	Sales	3.829	.159	576.877	1	.000	46.038
	Profit	10.944	.401	743.635	1	.000	56609.904
	Constant	-.877	.031	824.236	1	.000	.416

a. Variable(s) entered on step 1: Sales, Profit.

The equation allows us to estimate whether a brand has a "winning" season, based on actual metrics.

Let's evaluate the predictions based on a grid of possible sales gains and profit changes.

Annual Wins

Sales Change	Annual Pre-Tax Profit									
	-20.0%	-16.0%	-12.0%	-8.0%	-4.0%	0.0%	4.0%	8.0%	12.0%	16.0%
50.0%	4	5	7	9	10	12	13	14	15	15
45.0%	3	5	6	8	10	11	13	14	14	15
40.0%	3	4	5	7	9	11	12	13	14	15
35.0%	2	3	5	6	8	10	11	13	14	14
30.0%	2	3	4	6	7	9	11	12	13	14
25.0%	2	3	4	5	7	8	10	12	13	14
20.0%	1	2	3	4	6	8	9	11	12	13
15.0%	1	2	3	4	5	7	9	10	12	13
10.0%	1	2	2	3	5	6	8	10	11	12
5.0%	1	1	2	3	4	5	7	9	10	12
0.0%	1	1	2	2	3	5	6	8	10	11
-5.0%	1	1	1	2	3	4	6	7	9	11
-10.0%	0	1	1	2	2	4	5	6	8	10
-15.0%	0	1	1	1	2	3	4	6	7	9
-20.0%	0	1	1	1	2	3	4	5	7	8

Think of the table this way. An "average" year is one where you earn eight wins. Sales growth of 35% coupled with a pre-tax profit loss of 4% is considered an "average" year, like an NFL team with an 8-8 record. Similarly, 45% sale growth and a -8% pre-tax loss aligns with an 8-8 record.

A "playoff" season might include 10 wins. Sales growth of 5% coupled with 12% pre-tax profit is considered a 10-win season … a record of 10-6. If your business aligns with a 10-6 record, your business is like an NFL playoff team.

A "championship season" might align with 12 wins. Sales growth of 15% coupled with 12% pre-tax profit is considered a 12-win season … a record of 12-4.

What gets a CEO fired? How about a 5% sales drop coupled with a break-even year? The grid above suggests a 4-12 record, and in the NFL, a coach is likely to get fired if a 4-12 record is posted (unless it is the first year of a rebuilding project).

The grid, then, allows us to compare years. We can see if our business is winning or losing.

Here is how the model fitted to Chico's data.

Chicos						Equation	Equation
Year	Net Sales	Pre-Tax $	PreTax %	N/S Growth	Profit Rate	Wins	Losses
2001	$259,446	$45,772	17.6%				
2002	$378,085	$68,043	18.0%	0.457	0.180	15	1
2003	$531,108	$107,676	20.3%	0.405	0.203	15	1
2004	$768,499	$161,662	21.0%	0.447	0.210	15	1
2005	$1,066,882	$226,703	21.2%	0.388	0.212	15	1
2006	$1,640,927	$166,636	10.2%	0.538	0.102	15	1
2007	$1,714,326	$88,875	5.2%	0.045	0.052	7	9
2008	$1,582,405	($19,137)	-1.2%	-0.077	-0.012	3	13
2009	$1,713,150	$69,646	4.1%	0.083	0.041	8	8
2010	$1,904,954	$115,394	6.1%	0.112	0.061	9	7
2011	$2,196,360	$140,874	6.4%	0.153	0.064	10	6
2012	$2,581,057	$180,219	7.0%	0.175	0.070	10	6
2013	$2,586,037	$65,883	2.5%	0.002	0.025	6	10
2014	$2,675,211	$64,641	2.4%	0.034	0.024	6	10
2015	$2,642,309	$1,946	0.1%	-0.012	0.001	5	11

From 2002 to 2006, this was a Championship-level business! That's impressive performance.

In 2008, the bottom dropped out, yielding a year comparable to an NFL team going 3-13. Thanks, recession.

Then Management rebuilt the business. In 2011 and 2012, Chico's performed like a 10-6 NFL team, likely good enough to earn a spot in the playoff. But the last three years are not anything to write home about, are they?

Let's take a look at Macy's.

Macy's						Equation	Equation
Year	Net Sales	Pre-Tax $	PreTax %	N/S Growth	Profit Rate	Wins	Losses
2001	$15,785,000	$764,000	4.8%				
2002	$15,571,000	$1,048,000	6.7%	-0.014	0.067	7	9
2003	$15,412,000	$1,084,000	7.0%	-0.010	0.070	7	9
2004	$15,776,000	$1,116,000	7.1%	0.024	0.071	8	8
2005	$22,390,000	$2,044,000	9.1%	0.419	0.091	14	2
2006	$26,970,000	$1,446,000	5.4%	0.205	0.054	10	6
2007	$26,313,000	$1,320,000	5.0%	-0.024	0.050	6	10
2008	$24,892,000	($4,938,000)	-19.8%	-0.054	-0.198	1	15
2009	$23,489,000	$507,000	2.2%	-0.056	0.022	5	11
2010	$25,003,000	$1,320,000	5.3%	0.064	0.053	8	8
2011	$26,405,000	$1,968,000	7.5%	0.056	0.075	9	7
2012	$27,686,000	$2,102,000	7.6%	0.049	0.076	9	7
2013	$27,931,000	$2,290,000	8.2%	0.009	0.082	8	8
2014	$28,105,000	$2,390,000	8.5%	0.006	0.085	8	8
2015	$27,079,000	$1,678,000	6.2%	-0.037	0.062	7	9

2005 was a "Championship-level" year, as sales grew (likely due to an acquisition, but who cares, right?).

2008 was an unmitigated catastrophe. Macy's performed like an NFL with a 1-15 record.

Then the rebuilding process began, with an estimated 5-11 record in 2009, 8-8 in 2010, 9-7 in 2011, and 9-7 in 2012. In NFL parlance, Macy's performed almost well enough to earn a "Wild Card" spot in the playoffs. Clearly, however, Macy's did not perform at a Championship-level. The past three years yielded tepid 8-8, 8-8, and 7-9 records. Not surprisingly, Macy's made a change at the CEO level in 2016.

Here is the table for Nordstrom.

Nordstrom						Equation	Equation
Year	Net Sales	Pre-Tax $	PreTax %	N/S Growth	Profit Rate	Wins	Losses
2001	$5,607,687	$204,488	3.6%				
2002	$5,944,656	$195,624	3.3%	0.060	0.033	7	9
2003	$6,448,678	$398,141	6.2%	0.085	0.062	8	8
2004	$7,131,388	$647,281	9.1%	0.106	0.091	10	6
2005	$7,722,860	$885,225	11.5%	0.083	0.115	11	5
2006	$8,561,000	$1,149,000	13.4%	0.109	0.134	12	4
2007	$8,828,000	$1,247,000	14.1%	0.031	0.141	11	5
2008	$8,272,000	$779,000	9.4%	-0.063	0.094	8	8
2009	$8,258,000	$834,000	10.1%	-0.002	0.101	9	7
2010	$9,310,000	$1,118,000	12.0%	0.127	0.120	11	5
2011	$10,497,000	$1,249,000	11.9%	0.127	0.119	11	5
2012	$11,762,000	$1,345,000	11.4%	0.121	0.114	11	5
2013	$12,166,000	$1,350,000	11.1%	0.034	0.111	10	6
2014	$13,110,000	$1,323,000	10.1%	0.078	0.101	10	6
2015	$14,095,000	$1,101,000	7.8%	0.075	0.078	9	7

Look at the steady building process from 2002 (7-9) to 2003 (8-8), followed by playoff or Championship-level performances from 2004 – 2006. Then the dropoff begins in 2007 (11-5). In 2008, the business is at an 8-8 level (compare 8-8 to Macy's 1-15 performance in 2008 and the 3-13 record that Chico's posted in 2008).

The rebuilding process begins in 2009 (9-7), followed by three years of 11-5 performance between 2010 and 2012. Since 2012, performance is eroding, with a 9-7 outcome in 2015.

The methodology is almost magical. For mature businesses, we can evaluate how Management is performing. Once performance dips below an 8-8 level, we know the business is not as healthy as it should/could be. When the business dips down to a 6-10 or 5-11 or 4-12 level, changes need to be made.

Just as important, my friends, is the fact that it is rare for a business to "bounce back" within a year or two. Look at the Chico's table. The 3-13 record in 2008 rebounds, and then peaks in 2011. Look at the Macy's table. The 1-15 record in 2008 rebounds, and then peaks in 2012. Look at the Nordstrom table. The 8-8 record in 2008 rebounds, and then peaks in 2012. It takes time to rebuild a business.

Why go through this exercise?

When you are rebuilding a company or division or department, you have to find ways to tangibly communicate progress with employees. The vast majority of employees don't know how to calculate profit. Many employees understand that sales gains are good, but because they cannot calculate profit, they only focus on sales gains. And then there is a subset of the employee base (like me) that focus too much on profit, to the detriment of sales gains. Simply put, there has to be a way to communicate that a company is performing well, or is not performing well. There has to be a way to explain to employees that performance is unacceptable and needs to change.

When I took over the Circulation Department at Eddie Bauer, way back in the stone ages (1998), my division had posted a 5% sales decline and break-even profit performance. Let's look at our grid, and find out what those metrics translate to.

Annual Wins

Sales Change	Annual Pre-Tax Profit									
	-20.0%	-16.0%	-12.0%	-8.0%	-4.0%	0.0%	4.0%	8.0%	12.0%	16.0%
50.0%	4	5	7	9	10	12	13	14	15	15
45.0%	3	5	6	8	10	11	13	14	14	15
40.0%	3	4	5	7	9	11	12	13	14	15
35.0%	2	3	5	6	8	10	11	13	14	14
30.0%	2	3	4	6	7	9	11	12	13	14
25.0%	2	3	4	5	7	8	10	12	13	14
20.0%	1	2	3	4	6	8	9	11	12	13
15.0%	1	2	3	4	5	7	9	10	12	13
10.0%	1	2	2	3	5	6	8	10	11	12
5.0%	1	1	2	3	4	5	7	9	10	12
0.0%	1	1	2	2	3	5	6	8	10	11
-5.0%	1	1	1	2	3	4	6	7	9	11
-10.0%	0	1	1	2	2	4	5	6	8	10
-15.0%	0	1	1	1	2	3	4	6	7	9
-20.0%	0	1	1	1	2	3	4	5	7	8

Read across the -5% sales change row, read down the 0% pre-tax profit rate. What do you see?

I was taking over the Circulation responsibilities of a division that was performing like a 4-12 NFL team. Not good. Not good at all.

Here's what is interesting. When we "fixed" the online/catalog division at Eddie Bauer, we posted a 5% sales gain and 5% pre-tax profit. Read across the grid. What NFL record does that translate to?

It translates to a 7-9 NFL record … maybe 8-8 (since the table rounds values). "Fixing" the business was not "fixing" it by any credible definition. The "fix" yielded, at best, an average performing business. Did I earn a healthy bonus check that year? Yes! Did I deserve it? Probably not.

When I was hired to help fix Nordstrom.com, the online/catalog division had just posted a 5% sales gain and a -10% pre-tax profit rate. Let's look at the grid, once again.

Annual Wins

Sales Change	Annual Pre-Tax Profit									
	-20.0%	-16.0%	-12.0%	-8.0%	-4.0%	0.0%	4.0%	8.0%	12.0%	16.0%
50.0%	4	5	7	9	10	12	13	14	15	15
45.0%	3	5	6	8	10	11	13	14	14	15
40.0%	3	4	5	7	9	11	12	13	14	15
35.0%	2	3	5	6	8	10	11	13	14	14
30.0%	2	3	4	6	7	9	11	12	13	14
25.0%	2	3	4	5	7	8	10	12	13	14
20.0%	1	2	3	4	6	8	9	11	12	13
15.0%	1	2	3	4	5	7	9	10	12	13
10.0%	1	2	2	3	5	6	8	10	11	12
5.0%	1	1	2	3	4	5	7	9	10	12
0.0%	1	1	2	2	3	5	6	8	10	11
-5.0%	1	1	1	2	3	4	6	7	9	11
-10.0%	0	1	1	2	2	4	5	6	8	10
-15.0%	0	1	1	1	2	3	4	6	7	9
-20.0%	0	1	1	1	2	3	4	5	7	8

Read across the 5% sales gain row. Read down the -8% pre-tax profit column. You see a 3-13 record. Read down the -12% pre-tax profit column. You see a 2-14 record. That is AWFUL performance, don't you think? In other words, the business was somewhere between 2-14 and 3-13.

I didn't have this tool to explain performance to my staff, or to anybody. When hired, I inherited a team, as did most of my peers. It was terribly hard to explain to anybody just how awful our performance was. You'd think that telling people we just lost $30,000,000 for the second-consecutive year would result in a couple thousand employees running around with hair on fire. Nope. Nobody seemed to care. Sharing sales data or profit data didn't inspire employees to change.

I did have this tool when working with a recent client. This client was struggling. Really, really struggling! No matter how many ways I tried to illustrate this fact ("your customer acquisition efforts are failing" / "your annual twelve-month buyer repurchase rates are failing" / "you aren't growing sales or profit"), nobody listened.

So I tried a different tactic. I plugged sales/profit data into the grid. Then, in a write-up to the Executive Team, I told the Executive Team that they were performing like a 4-12 NFL team. Worse, I told them that their performance came off of a year when they performed like a 5-11 NFL team. Finally, I told the Executive Team that I did not see a way out of the mess in the short-term, in spite of all of the improvements they were trying to implement.

For years, the client didn't necessarily "hear" what I was saying.

I sent the paper to the client at about 4:00pm in the afternoon.

The next morning, by 9:00am, I received a call from a member of the Executive Team.

Executive: "What is *this*?"

Kevin: "What is *what*?"

Executive: "You said we perform like a 4-12 NFL team?"

Kevin: "No, I said you perform like a 4-12 NFL team coming off of a 5-11 season."

Executive: "That means we are *awful*."

Kevin: "Correct."

Executive: "But we aren't awful. We are a great brand."

Kevin: "You are like the Dallas Cowboys suffering through a 4-12 season."

Executive: "We aren't that bad."

Kevin: "Yes, you are."

Executive: "But other companies are performing at the same level, so it can't be us."

Kevin: "There are other 4-12 teams in the NFL, too."

Executive: "Do you have clients that perform like 12-4 NFL teams?"

Kevin: "Absolutely."

Executive: "Oh."

When I worked at Eddie Bauer (way back in the stone ages) Management communicated that Eddie Bauer could not post 10% pre-tax profit, because their "*business model was different*". Nonsense. The company was comfortable posting 8-8 records when business was good, and didn't want to do what was necessary to be great.

By following simple fundamentals, it is not hard to take a business from 4-12 to 8-8.

It is hard to take a business from 8-8 to 12-4. Look at the Macy's example, once again.

Macy's						Equation	Equation
Year	Net Sales	Pre-Tax $	PreTax %	N/S Growth	Profit Rate	Wins	Losses
2001	$15,785,000	$764,000	4.8%				
2002	$15,571,000	$1,048,000	6.7%	-0.014	0.067	7	9
2003	$15,412,000	$1,084,000	7.0%	-0.010	0.070	7	9
2004	$15,776,000	$1,116,000	7.1%	0.024	0.071	8	8
2005	$22,390,000	$2,044,000	9.1%	0.419	0.091	14	2
2006	$26,970,000	$1,446,000	5.4%	0.205	0.054	10	6
2007	$26,313,000	$1,320,000	5.0%	-0.024	0.050	6	10
2008	$24,892,000	($4,938,000)	-19.8%	-0.054	-0.198	1	15
2009	$23,489,000	$507,000	2.2%	-0.056	0.022	5	11
2010	$25,003,000	$1,320,000	5.3%	0.064	0.053	8	8
2011	$26,405,000	$1,968,000	7.5%	0.056	0.075	9	7
2012	$27,686,000	$2,102,000	7.6%	0.049	0.076	9	7
2013	$27,931,000	$2,290,000	8.2%	0.009	0.082	8	8
2014	$28,105,000	$2,390,000	8.5%	0.006	0.085	8	8
2015	$27,079,000	$1,678,000	6.2%	-0.037	0.062	7	9

Macy's came out of the 1-15 year of 2008, improved to 5-11, then to 8-8. And that's about it. Trade journalists lauded Macy's for exceptional "omnichannel" performance. But sales didn't grow much, and the quality of profit was not great. Everybody was cheering for "average" performance. If Macy's wanted to be "great", they would have innovated or executed at a 12-4 level, right?

We now have a framework for evaluating "great" performance.

I know, I know, you work at Wal-Mart, and the best you can ever hope to achieve is 4% pre-tax profit, or whatever. Fine. Adjust the equation for your business model. Same with Best Buy. But create your own grid, and clearly communicate how lousy your performance actually is when business isn't good.

Now that you have this framework, why not do what sports teams do?

In other words, why not create banners that you "hang from the rafters"? Anytime you have a 10-6 year, you "made the playoffs". Hang a banner! Anytime you have a 12-4 year or better, you "won a championship". Hang a banner!!!

At Chico's, you would hang championship banners for 2001 – 2006. You'd hang playoff banners for 2011 and 2012. And you'd clearly communicate to every employee at Chico's that you've made the playoffs in just two of the past nine years. You are not "winning", are you?

At Macy's, you would hang a championship banner for 2004. You'd hang a playoff banner for 2005. And you'd clearly communicate to every employee at Macy's that you have not made the playoffs in a decade. You are not "winning", are you? Macy's performs like the Detroit Lions.

At Nordstrom, you would hang a championship banner for 2006. You'd hang playoff banners for 2004, 2005, 2007, 2010, 2011, 2012, 2013, and 2014. You are the New England Patriots, for crying out loud!!! And you'd clearly communicate to every employee at Nordstrom that performance has dropped off … Nordstrom is no longer a playoff caliber business.

Alright. Remember the graphs for Green Bay and for Detroit, earlier in the chapter? Here are comparable charts for Chico's, Macy's, and Nordstrom. We'll start with Chico's.

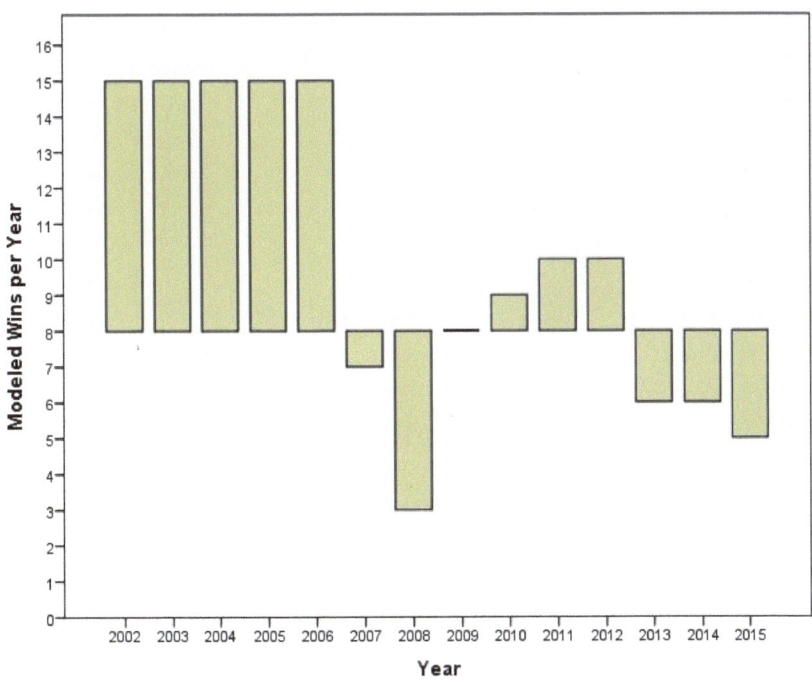

We can see the three year rebuild that Chico's enjoyed (2010, 2011, 2012), followed by tepid performance thereafter. This business will be rebuilt once again. In fact, retail brands perform an awful lot like sports teams, when viewed via this framework.

This is the graph for Macy's.

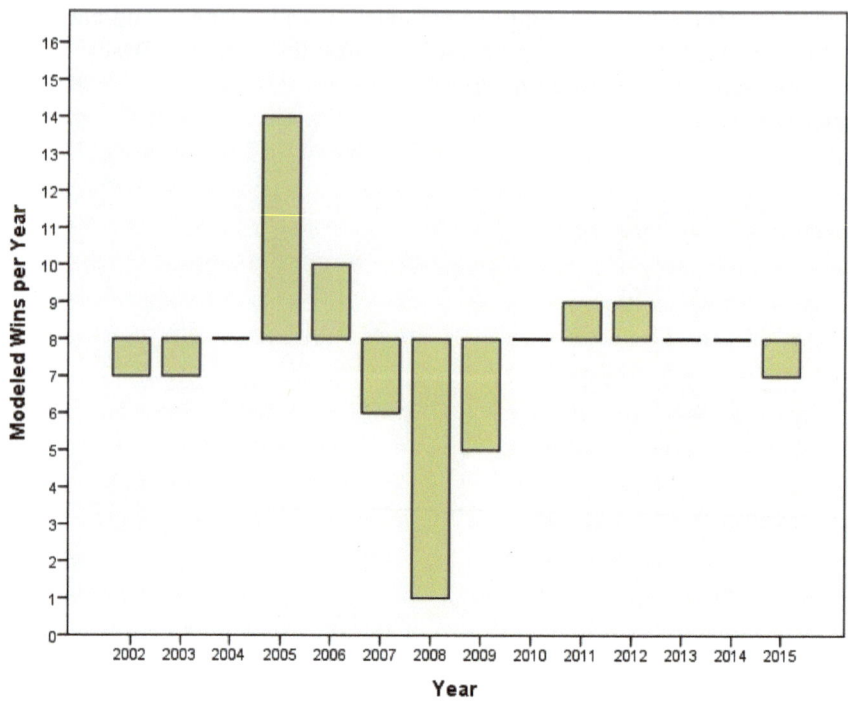

Graphically, this is an 8-8 team, isn't it? We can see how the business was harmed by the Great Recession. But in the past six years? Not much of a recovery. Macy's can return to average performance. It will probably require a different strategy to break through to "playoff" performance.

Here is the graph for Nordstrom.

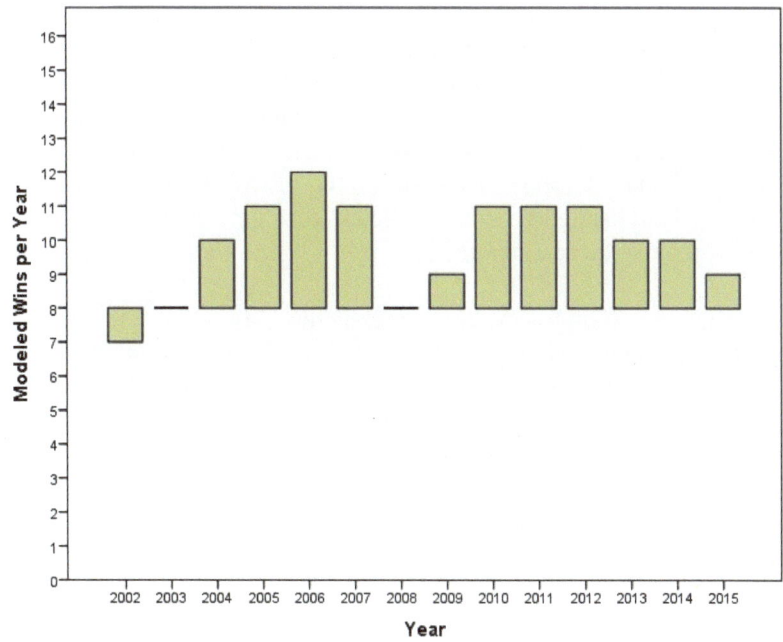

This graph looks different than the other two graphs. We observe a brand that built steadily and slowly – hit a pothole during The Great Recession, then rebounded. Take the recession out of the story, and you sense that an era is ending at Nordstrom, don't you? Without the recession, the curve represents a quadratic function with a peak that should have happened around 2008. One senses that a new strategy might have to be employed, to push Nordstrom back to levels from the 2006 timeframe.

When we look at each business through this framework, it becomes obvious that Chico's is most in need of a rebuild.

Does the framework make sense?

Say you were the new CEO at Chico's. The graphs and data show that it will take 2-3 years to rebuild a business. The CEO can communicate the timeframe required to fix the business. The CEO can use the framework to demonstrate that progress is being made. Best of all, the framework can be more easily understood than typical sales/profit metrics. Too few employees related to sales/profit metrics. Many employees understand wins and losses.

When the new CEO communicates to her new team, she uses the framework to argue that the company has had "losing seasons". She uses this argument because she is going to need staff to align with her vision for the future. Too often, employees don't want to change. Employees like doing their job the way they've always done their job. It is helpful to explain that doing the job the way the job has always been done yields a 6-10 record – a losing record – a record that gets people fired. The framework makes the case for change.

Conversely, the framework may make the case for not blowing something up. Think about Lands' End for a moment. In 2014, the company would have posted an approximate 8-8 record (they publish adjusted earnings and not clear EBT and they wrote down the value of the brand, making comparisons more challenging). They made a Leadership change, and tried to become more fashion-centric. According to their financial documents, 2015 performance falls to 5-11. Through much of 2016, performance falls further, approaching 4-12 levels. Needless to say, going from 8-8 to 5-11 to 4-12 is not good. The CEO was relieved of her duties in 2016. One could argue that blowing up the core business was the right decision for the long-term. One could argue (opposite) that the core business had to be protected. The data shows that the company spent two years going from average performance to terrible performance. It will take several years to construct a rebuild.

Rebuilds are hard. There is no guarantee that a rebuild will be successful. Let's look at JCP as an example. The business was blown-up a half-decade ago, following a 5-11 (after using EBITDA-reconciled calculations) year in 2011. We all know what happened after that. My calculations suggest a 1-15 performance in 2012, a 2-14 performance in 2013, and then 6-10 and 7-9 performances in 2014 and 2015. The process can be long, and superior performance may not be achieved. I realize that JCP is getting positive press right now. But JCP has not come close to making up the sales lost during the 1-15 / 2-14 years of 2011 / 2012.

In general, I try to use Net Sales and EBT (earnings before taxes) to perform my calculations. Not every company releases EBT in their 10-K statements, some use reconciliation techniques. Regardless, by using something close to EBT, we can make common comparisons over time.

Alright, that's a lot of information. My goal was to demonstrate that we can align profit and loss metrics with wins, allowing us to view the performance of a retail and/or e-commerce brand similarly to the won/lost record in the National Football League.

What Went Wrong?

If we want to rebuild a business, we should probably know what went wrong, don't you think?

I like to use what I call a "comp segment" framework to diagnose why the business is not performing to expectations. My comp segment analysis is comprised of two tables – with many variants of the first table.

The first table analyzes how customers with exactly two purchases in the past year perform in the next month. The query is simple. I select all customers who purchased exactly two times in the past year. Then, I measure how much these customers spent across all channels and all product lines in the next month. This analysis is repeated, subtracting one month from the query dates, for the past three years (you can go back as many years as you like).

This is what the comp segment analysis looks like for an actual e-commerce brand.

2x Comp Segment Analysis - Overall Results					
	This Year	Last Year	2 Yrs Ago	TY vs. LY	LY vs. 2Y	TY vs. 2YR
August	$8.45	$7.38	$7.10	14.5%	4.0%	19.1%
July	$6.97	$8.81	$7.69	-20.9%	14.5%	-9.5%
June	$8.42	$9.64	$7.61	-12.6%	26.6%	10.7%
May	$9.88	$7.33	$9.10	34.8%	-19.5%	8.5%
April	$7.43	$7.47	$7.56	-0.4%	-1.3%	-1.7%
March	$9.45	$8.39	$9.36	12.5%	-10.4%	0.9%
February	$6.12	$5.10	$4.98	20.0%	2.3%	22.8%
January	$4.69	$4.93	$5.12	-4.9%	-3.7%	-8.4%
December	$8.54	$8.93	$7.00	-4.4%	27.5%	22.0%
November	$8.19	$7.28	$6.67	12.5%	9.3%	22.9%
October	$7.10	$5.23	$5.19	35.6%	0.9%	36.8%
September	$7.64	$6.54	$6.74	16.9%	-3.0%	13.4%
Totals	$92.88	$87.03	$84.12	6.7%	3.5%	10.4%

I first look at the "Totals" row. On an annual basis, I can see that something good is happening (in this example). The comp segment framework seeks to eliminate bias, though no technique is going to eliminate all biases. The framework does a reasonable job of eliminating the impact of marketing, mostly because all customers purchased twice in the past year and are reasonably "equal". If promotional rhythm changes significantly, then the methodology will be marginally biased. If creative strategies change significantly, then the methodology will detect the changes (if changes helped/hurt sales) and assign the changes to what I call "merchandise productivity".

Let's look at the impact of promotions. This table isolates orders that were attached to a free shipping code.

2x Comp Segment Analysis - Orders With Free Shipping						
	This Year	Last Year	2 Yrs Ago	TY vs. LY	LY vs. 2Y	TY vs. 2YR
August	$5.40	$5.31	$5.29	1.8%	0.4%	2.2%
July	$5.09	$4.81	$5.49	5.8%	-12.4%	-7.3%
June	$6.18	$5.47	$5.31	13.1%	2.9%	16.4%
May	$7.49	$4.38	$6.50	71.1%	-32.6%	15.3%
April	$5.40	$3.78	$5.52	43.1%	-31.6%	-2.1%
March	$7.58	$4.82	$7.43	57.4%	-35.2%	2.1%
February	$4.47	$3.62	$3.50	23.7%	3.2%	27.6%
January	$3.23	$3.34	$3.74	-3.1%	-10.8%	-13.6%
December	$6.21	$6.44	$4.98	-3.5%	29.3%	24.8%
November	$6.11	$5.41	$4.49	12.9%	20.5%	36.1%
October	$4.89	$3.82	$2.78	28.1%	37.7%	76.4%
September	$5.42	$4.94	$4.11	9.7%	20.2%	31.8%
Totals	$67.49	$56.12	$59.14	20.3%	-5.1%	14.1%

Look at what happened between February and June! Management "bought" merchandise productivity by offering discounts and promotions at high levels, after reducing free shipping during a comparable time the year prior.

This table shows what happened to orders not assigned a free shipping code.

2x Comp Segment Analysis - Orders Without Free Shipping

	This Year	Last Year	2 Yrs Ago	TY vs. LY	LY vs. 2Y	TY vs. 2YR
August	$3.05	$2.08	$1.81	46.9%	14.6%	68.4%
July	$1.88	$4.00	$2.21	-53.1%	81.4%	-14.9%
June	$2.24	$4.17	$2.30	-46.3%	81.3%	-2.6%
May	$2.39	$2.95	$2.61	-19.0%	13.3%	-8.2%
April	$2.03	$3.69	$2.04	-45.0%	80.8%	-0.6%
March	$1.87	$3.58	$1.94	-47.9%	84.8%	-3.6%
February	$1.64	$1.48	$1.48	11.2%	0.2%	11.4%
January	$1.45	$1.59	$1.37	-8.8%	15.9%	5.7%
December	$2.33	$2.49	$2.02	-6.5%	23.0%	15.0%
November	$2.08	$1.87	$2.17	11.2%	-13.9%	-4.2%
October	$2.20	$1.41	$2.41	56.1%	-41.5%	-8.7%
September	$2.22	$1.60	$2.62	39.0%	-39.2%	-15.5%
Totals	$25.38	$30.91	$24.98	-17.9%	23.7%	1.6%

Yup – Management is cheating! If I were the new CEO of this business, I'd have a strike against me. I have to figure out how to grow sales without the benefit of incremental free shipping promotions. This is going to make the rebuild of the business more difficult, isn't it?

In this table, I analyze existing merchandise – items that existed for at least twelve months prior to the date the customer purchased the item.

2x Comp Segment Analysis - Existing Items

	This Year	Last Year	2 Yrs Ago	TY vs. LY	LY vs. 2Y	TY vs. 2YR
August	$7.00	$5.49	$5.51	27.4%	-0.3%	27.0%
July	$5.49	$6.61	$5.84	-17.0%	13.2%	-6.0%
June	$7.41	$6.30	$6.47	17.6%	-2.6%	14.5%
May	$7.41	$6.19	$7.85	19.7%	-21.1%	-5.5%
April	$5.24	$6.02	$6.48	-13.0%	-7.0%	-19.2%
March	$7.19	$6.45	$8.46	11.5%	-23.8%	-15.1%
February	$4.53	$3.87	$4.66	17.1%	-17.0%	-2.8%
January	$3.50	$3.53	$4.84	-0.9%	-27.1%	-27.8%
December	$5.83	$6.26	$6.60	-6.9%	-5.1%	-11.6%
November	$5.94	$5.21	$6.19	14.1%	-15.9%	-4.0%
October	$4.90	$4.20	$4.64	16.7%	-9.6%	5.5%
September	$5.74	$5.43	$5.90	5.8%	-8.0%	-2.7%
Totals	$70.17	$65.56	$73.44	7.0%	-10.7%	-4.4%

There are gains in productivity – but remember, the gains align with free shipping promotions, not with organic growth. Today, existing items are performing four percent worse than two years ago. The rebuild will require an evaluation of the existing merchandise assortment.

Here is the same table for new merchandise.

2x Comp Segment Analysis - New Items						
	This Year	Last Year	2 Yrs Ago	TY vs. LY	LY vs. 2Y	TY vs. 2YR
August	$1.46	$1.89	$1.59	-23.0%	19.0%	-8.4%
July	$1.48	$2.20	$1.85	-32.9%	18.7%	-20.3%
June	$1.02	$3.34	$1.14	-69.5%	192.2%	-11.0%
May	$2.47	$1.13	$1.26	117.4%	-9.8%	96.2%
April	$2.20	$1.44	$1.08	52.2%	33.1%	102.6%
March	$2.26	$1.95	$0.90	16.0%	116.3%	150.9%
February	$1.59	$1.23	$0.32	29.2%	285.3%	397.9%
January	$1.19	$1.40	$0.28	-15.0%	403.3%	327.7%
December	$2.71	$2.67	$0.40	1.5%	560.3%	570.5%
November	$2.25	$2.08	$0.47	8.4%	338.3%	375.1%
October	$2.20	$1.04	$0.55	112.3%	90.2%	303.8%
September	$1.90	$1.11	$0.84	71.3%	32.3%	126.6%
Totals	$22.70	$21.47	$10.68	5.8%	101.0%	112.5%

Management made significant changes to the merchandise assortment, didn't they? They heavily invested in new items, and yet, in the past year, the business grew mostly because of the impact of free shipping promotions. Fortunately, this is a story that I don't always get to see. In most of my projects, Management reduces the number of new items over time, and this causes a whole series of problems.

I also evaluate marketing channels. In this table, I evaluate the performance of email marketing over the past three years.

2x Comp Segment Analysis - Email Marketing						
	This Year	Last Year	2 Yrs Ago	TY vs. LY	LY vs. 2Y	TY vs. 2YR
August	$1.81	$1.25	$0.89	44.7%	41.1%	104.2%
July	$1.20	$2.89	$0.90	-58.5%	220.2%	32.8%
June	$2.16	$1.79	$1.78	20.7%	0.3%	21.1%
May	$2.59	$0.63	$1.44	312.4%	-56.5%	79.5%
April	$1.41	$0.70	$0.60	101.3%	17.5%	136.5%
March	$2.85	$2.18	$3.31	30.8%	-34.1%	-13.7%
February	$1.46	$0.68	$0.80	115.7%	-15.7%	81.9%
January	$0.41	$0.53	$0.58	-22.6%	-8.5%	-29.2%
December	$1.45	$2.55	$1.66	-43.0%	54.1%	-12.2%
November	$2.78	$2.37	$2.36	17.3%	0.8%	18.2%
October	$1.40	$0.73	$0.91	93.0%	-20.4%	53.6%
September	$2.46	$2.09	$1.92	17.4%	9.1%	28.1%
Totals	$21.99	$18.40	$17.15	19.5%	7.3%	28.3%

Notice the huge increases in April and May. I like to compare email marketing performance to free shipping performance. The correlation between this table and the free shipping table tells me that email marketing is not necessarily working better than in the past, but rather, Management elected to use email marketing to announce free shipping promotions.

This tells me that the marketing team does not have merchandising chops, or that Management was desperate to grow sales. Regardless, I always want to see email demand growth independent of discounts and promotions. The rebuilding process will likely require a reduction in promotions, which will drive down the productivity of email marketing, which will cause a lot of employees to be frustrated with the rebuilding process. These issues need to be addresses ahead of time, and communicated clearly to all employees, so that expectations are set properly.

Look at the paid search table.

2x Comp Segment Analysis - Paid Search						
	This Year	Last Year	2 Yrs Ago	TY vs. LY	LY vs. 2Y	TY vs. 2YR
August	$0.01	$0.02	$0.03	-50.7%	-22.2%	-61.7%
July	$0.01	$0.00	$0.02	205.5%	-86.4%	-58.4%
June	$0.02	$0.00	$0.01	1134.3%	-88.9%	37.1%
May	$0.01	$0.01	$0.03	26.7%	-73.5%	-66.4%
April	$0.01	$0.01	$0.01	7.8%	12.9%	21.7%
March	$0.01	$0.01	$0.06	24.7%	-86.2%	-82.8%
February	$0.00	$0.01	$0.02	-100.0%	-68.2%	-100.0%
January	$0.01	$0.01	$0.02	36.6%	-64.3%	-51.2%
December	$0.00	$0.03	$0.05	-100.0%	-38.0%	-100.0%
November	$0.02	$0.01	$0.07	93.4%	-85.7%	-72.4%
October	$0.00	$0.02	$0.03	-100.0%	-38.2%	-100.0%
September	$0.02	$0.01	$0.02	69.1%	-35.4%	9.2%
Totals	$0.12	$0.14	$0.38	-12.4%	-63.3%	-67.9%

This brand is de-emphasizing the paid search program, and is generating very little volume as a consequence. The rebuilding process will require a thorough evaluation of prior paid search activities, in order to understand why this brand is not leveraging this important marketing channel.

I typically run tables for each merchandise category. I want to see if there are categories that are struggling, and categories that are exceeding the company average. Here, the second largest merchandise category is under-performing the overall average, and will need to be addressed.

2x Comp Segment Analysis - 2nd Most Important Category					
	This Year	Last Year	2 Yrs Ago	TY vs. LY	LY vs. 2Y	TY vs. 2YR
August	$0.82	$0.61	$0.59	34.2%	4.1%	39.7%
July	$0.73	$0.62	$0.59	16.9%	6.1%	24.0%
June	$0.75	$0.61	$0.99	23.7%	-38.6%	-24.1%
May	$0.66	$0.78	$0.91	-15.7%	-14.2%	-27.7%
April	$0.79	$0.68	$0.66	16.5%	3.0%	20.0%
March	$0.77	$0.71	$1.12	8.3%	-36.9%	-31.7%
February	$0.50	$0.67	$0.63	-25.7%	6.4%	-20.9%
January	$0.54	$0.61	$0.63	-11.4%	-4.1%	-15.1%
December	$0.88	$1.21	$0.93	-27.1%	30.8%	-4.7%
November	$1.06	$0.75	$0.44	41.4%	70.3%	140.8%
October	$0.55	$0.58	$0.60	-5.0%	-3.8%	-8.7%
September	$0.70	$0.55	$0.35	28.6%	57.1%	102.0%
Totals	$8.75	$8.38	$8.44	4.5%	-0.7%	3.7%

The 2x comp segment table framework can be (and should be) run for different price points, merchandise categories, marketing channels, geographic regions, you name it. The framework tells the Leader where attention needs to be focused.

Maybe the most important table is the second table mentioned earlier … measuring the number of new + reactivated customers.

Number of New + Reactivated Customers					
	This Year	Last Year	2 Yrs Ago	TY vs. LY	LY vs. 2Y	IY vs. 2YR
August	3,540	3,378	3,838	4.8%	-12.0%	-7.8%
July	3,430	4,217	4,375	-18.7%	-3.6%	-21.6%
June	4,160	4,562	4,910	-8.8%	-7.1%	-15.3%
May	5,082	4,399	5,266	15.5%	-16.5%	-3.5%
April	4,101	4,150	4,495	-1.2%	-7.7%	-8.8%
March	4,137	3,757	4,771	10.1%	-21.3%	-13.3%
February	3,115	2,297	3,115	35.6%	-26.3%	0.0%
January	2,351	2,530	2,807	-7.1%	-9.9%	-16.2%
December	6,866	7,169	6,607	-4.2%	8.5%	3.9%
November	3,722	4,168	4,587	-10.7%	-9.1%	-18.9%
October	3,482	3,174	3,621	9.7%	-12.3%	-3.8%
September	3,592	3,724	3,900	-3.5%	-4.5%	-7.9%
Totals	47,578	47,525	52,292	0.1%	-9.1%	-9.0%

#OhBoy.

New + Reactivated counts are generally flat in the past year, but are down 9% from two years ago.

I've analyzed more than two-hundred brands since founding MineThatData. Across my entire client base, the average annual repurchase rate among twelve-month buyers is 37%. That's it. Thirty-seven of one-hundred customers will purchase again, requiring sixty-three new + reactivated buyers to replenish the customer file.

Remember that this company is heavily leveraging free shipping promotions. This makes it very likely that true new + reactivated counts would be in decline in the past year as well. This company/brand is covering up merchandising sins and new + reactivated customer sins with promotions. If I were named CEO, I would have two tough challenges to address. I would have to figure out how to grow merchandise productivity independent of promotions, and I would have to figure out how to increase new + reactivated buyer counts independent of promotions.

The tables help me understand the areas of the business I need to address.

I also run a repurchase table, to understand how customer behavior has changed over the past two years. Here is a sample table. The definition of new + reactivated in this table is a bit different – instead of measuring incremental monthly counts, the table measures annual counts and uses a different window for determining new + reactivated – hence the increase in customers.

Annual Retention Metrics

Widgets International

	This Year	Last Year	Change
Beginning Buyers	61,345	61,081	0.4%
Annual Repurchase Rate	31.1%	30.2%	3.0%
Orders per Buyer	1.645	1.633	0.7%
Items per Order	4.425	4.458	-0.8%
Price per Item Purchased	$25.72	$26.12	-1.5%
Average Order Value	$113.80	$116.45	-2.3%
Demand per Buyer	$187.21	$190.16	-1.6%
Demand per Inventory	$58.25	$57.44	1.4%
New + Reactivated Buyers	47,843	42,896	11.5%
Orders per Buyer	1.203	1.195	0.7%
Items per Order	3.693	3.653	1.1%
Price per Item Purchased	$28.38	$29.46	-3.6%
Average Order Value	$104.82	$107.61	-2.6%
Demand per Buyer	$126.06	$128.57	-2.0%
Beginning Buyers	61,345	61,081	0.4%
Annual Repurchase Rate	31.1%	30.2%	3.0%
Active Buyers	19,087	18,449	3.5%
New + Reactivated Buyers	47,843	42,896	11.5%
End of Year Buyers	66,930	61,345	9.1%
12 Month Buyers 2 Years Ago	61,081		
12 Month Buyers Last Year	61,345	0.4%	
12 Month Buyers Today	66,930	9.1%	

This table suggests that the customer file is nine percent bigger today than two years ago, so at least that is a positive story. Regardless, a lot of business in the past year was "purchased" via free shipping. As a new CEO, I want to challenge my team to grow the business without discounts and promotions.

Notice that the repurchase rate is reasonably constant, orders per buyer are reasonably constant, items per order are reasonably constant, and price per item purchased is reasonably constant. This business is mostly "static" or "stuck". Management has not been able to find anything outside of free shipping promotions to grow the business. As a new CEO, I would have a lot of work to do to find avenues for growth.

I combine my comp segment framework with my wins/losses framework. Here is how the business evolved over the past five years.

Year	Net Sales	Pre-Tax %	NS Incr	Wins	Losses
2010	$24,307,798	8.3%			
2011	$26,605,897	1.5%	9.5%	7	9
2012	$24,456,975	3.7%	-8.1%	5	11
2013	$20,048,019	7.3%	-18.0%	5	11
2014	$19,208,708	10.1%	-4.2%	8	8
2015	$18,046,778	6.3%	-6.0%	6	10

Look at Net Sales. This business stopped growing in 2012, and has been in decline ever since. The declines in top-line growth have been largely overcome by increases in pre-tax profit rates, until 2015. We can see that Management "bought" sales in 2011, but harmed profitability in the process. As Management fixed the sins of 2011, the won/lost record reflected the sales decline. Once pre-tax profit hit reasonable levels, the won/lost record improved.

Still, this is a 6-10 business. Our analytics tell us that net sales declines were mitigated with free shipping promotions, and those promotions (which our tables suggested did not exist the year prior) probably cost the business significant pre-tax profit.

The current Management team took this business as far as they could. They greatly increased the assortment of new merchandise, which may well help the business a few years from now as new items become highly productive winning items. But to try to grow, Management went back to free shipping promotions that hurt profitability. As a result, this business is as healthy as an NFL franchise with a 6-10 record and a five year run without any playoff appearances.

This business needs to embark on a rebuilding project.

We can estimate what the metrics need to look like for this business to be a "playoff caliber" team. What if we keep net sales flat in 2016, and keep profit flat?

Year	Net Sales	Pre-Tax %	NS Incr	Wins	Losses
2010	$24,307,798	8.3%			
2011	$26,605,897	1.5%	9.5%	7	9
2012	$24,456,975	3.7%	-8.1%	5	11
2013	$20,048,019	7.3%	-18.0%	5	11
2014	$19,208,708	10.1%	-4.2%	8	8
2015	$18,046,778	6.3%	-6.0%	6	10
2016	$18,046,778	6.3%	0.0%	7	9

That's not good enough, is it?

How about if net sales increase to nineteen million dollars, and profit remains flat?

Year	Net Sales	Pre-Tax %	NS Incr	Wins	Losses
2010	$24,307,798	8.3%			
2011	$26,605,897	1.5%	9.5%	7	9
2012	$24,456,975	3.7%	-8.1%	5	11
2013	$20,048,019	7.3%	-18.0%	5	11
2014	$19,208,708	10.1%	-4.2%	8	8
2015	$18,046,778	6.3%	-6.0%	6	10
2016	$19,000,000	6.3%	5.3%	8	8

That's better, but still not good enough.

How about if net sales increase to twenty million dollars, and profit remains flat?

Year	Net Sales	Pre-Tax %	NS Incr	Wins	Losses
2010	$24,307,798	8.3%			
2011	$26,605,897	1.5%	9.5%	7	9
2012	$24,456,975	3.7%	-8.1%	5	11
2013	$20,048,019	7.3%	-18.0%	5	11
2014	$19,208,708	10.1%	-4.2%	8	8
2015	$18,046,778	6.3%	-6.0%	6	10
2016	$20,000,000	6.3%	10.8%	9	7

Things are getting better. How about holding profit flat, but getting to twenty-one million in annual sales?

Year	Net Sales	Pre-Tax %	NS Incr	Wins	Losses
2010	$24,307,798	8.3%			
2011	$26,605,897	1.5%	9.5%	7	9
2012	$24,456,975	3.7%	-8.1%	5	11
2013	$20,048,019	7.3%	-18.0%	5	11
2014	$19,208,708	10.1%	-4.2%	8	8
2015	$18,046,778	6.3%	-6.0%	6	10
2016	$21,000,000	6.3%	16.4%	10	6

Each five percent increase in net sales, if profit rate holds constant (and that is hard to do), yields an additional "win" in NFL terms. In order for this to be a healthy business that is "playoff caliber", the business must grow by 16% coupled with flat profit rates at 6.3% of net sales.

The latter is hard to do, if sales increase.

Let's go back to the example where net sales are nineteen million dollars.

Year	Net Sales	Pre-Tax %	NS Incr	Wins	Losses
2010	$24,307,798	8.3%			
2011	$26,605,897	1.5%	9.5%	7	9
2012	$24,456,975	3.7%	-8.1%	5	11
2013	$20,048,019	7.3%	-18.0%	5	11
2014	$19,208,708	10.1%	-4.2%	8	8
2015	$18,046,778	6.3%	-6.0%	6	10
2016	$19,000,000	6.3%	5.3%	8	8

This gets us to an average business, with an 8-8 record.

What happens if pre-tax profit improves from 6.3% of net sales to 7.8% of net sales?

Year	Net Sales	Pre-Tax %	NS Incr	Wins	Losses
2010	$24,307,798	8.3%			
2011	$26,605,897	1.5%	9.5%	7	9
2012	$24,456,975	3.7%	-8.1%	5	11
2013	$20,048,019	7.3%	-18.0%	5	11
2014	$19,208,708	10.1%	-4.2%	8	8
2015	$18,046,778	6.3%	-6.0%	6	10
2016	$19,000,000	7.8%	5.3%	9	7

Now what happens if pre-tax profit improves from 7.8% of net sales to 10% of net sales?

Year	Net Sales	Pre-Tax %	NS Incr	Wins	Losses
2010	$24,307,798	8.3%			
2011	$26,605,897	1.5%	9.5%	7	9
2012	$24,456,975	3.7%	-8.1%	5	11
2013	$20,048,019	7.3%	-18.0%	5	11
2014	$19,208,708	10.1%	-4.2%	8	8
2015	$18,046,778	6.3%	-6.0%	6	10
2016	$19,000,000	10.0%	5.3%	10	6

In other words, each 1.8 point increase in pre-tax profit rate equates to one additional "win" in NFL terms.

I have two dimensions I can work around. Each 5.0 point increase in net sales adds one "win" in NFL terms. Each 1.8 point increase in pre-tax profit adds one "win" in NFL terms. If I am going to be the new CEO, then I know that I need "four wins" to achieve a healthy business. Either sales have to increase by twenty points, pre-tax profit has to improve by 7.2 points, or any combination thereof. If I am the new CEO, then I have a lot of work to do, don't I? And I cannot allow either metric to slide, or then the other metric has to compensate even more for the loss.

This means I need to sit down with my Finance Team, and express what I need to accomplish to achieve a healthy business. Within two years, I probably need to grow net sales by 10% (reversing a four year sales decline, so that won't be easy) and yield a pre-tax profit rate of about 10%. If both goals are achieved in two years, then the business is healthy and is equal to an NFL team that achieves a 10-6 record and earns a playoff spot.

Clearly, I'm not going to be able to cheat or manufacture fake growth. Discounts and promotions are going to hurt pre-tax profit rates, making it harder to build a healthy business. To be honest, our analytics indicated that growth was manufactured with free shipping promotions, so the new CEO has been put in a difficult spot.

Setting Up a Winning Plan

Seldom does one get to take over a "winning" business. It's far more common for the new Leader to inherit a struggling business. When inheriting a struggling business, it is important to understand the dynamics surrounding the struggling business.

In this booklet, we analyzed a business with a twelve-month buyer file possessing an approximate 31% annual repurchase rate. This means that for every 100 customers who purchase in 2015, just 31 will purchase again in 2016.

The new CEO needs to understand the process a customer goes through, from a first purchase to a loyal customer. Opaque measures like lifetime value help to some extent, but do not make clear the strategic changes a CEO must implement.

For the business we are analyzing, here are cumulative repurchase rates by month by life stage.

Cumulative Repurchase Rates				
Month	1x - 2x	2x - 3x	3x - 4x	4x - 5x
0	3.6%	5.4%	6.6%	7.4%
1	7.4%	12.3%	15.3%	18.1%
2	9.6%	16.5%	21.4%	24.4%
3	11.5%	19.8%	26.0%	29.9%
6	15.4%	27.2%	35.9%	41.7%
12	21.2%	38.3%	49.8%	57.8%
24	26.9%	48.3%	61.4%	69.6%
36	29.9%	53.0%	66.6%	72.2%
48	31.6%	55.3%	67.3%	72.8%

When a customer purchases for the first time, the customer has a 21% chance of buying again within twelve months. That's not an uncommon situation, my friends. And look what happens after a fourth purchase – the customer has just a 58% chance of purchasing again within twelve months.

In other words, it takes a long time before a customer becomes a "loyal" customer.

Given these dynamics, the new CEO needs to focus the company on finding as many new customers as possible, for this is where growth will come from. Just as important, the new CEO must focus the company on finding low-cost or no-cost new customers.

Here is what five-year future value looks like for a first-time purchaser.

Future	Demand	Ad Cost	Profit
Year 1	$30.00	$8.00	$2.50
Year 2	$20.00	$5.00	$2.00
Year 3	$14.00	$3.00	$1.90
Year 4	$10.00	$2.00	$1.50
Year 5	$7.00	$1.00	$1.45
Totals	$81.00	$19.00	$9.35

As you can see, the customer only generates a bit more than nine dollars of profit over five years. Armed with this knowledge, the CEO can set goals and objectives surrounding new customer acquisition targets at low-cost / no-cost. With marginal long-term value, inexpensive customer acquisition programs are critical.

I recently worked with a CEO who managed a business similar to this example. The CEO tried valiantly to increase annual repurchase rates, to no avail. Loyalty program. Website optimization. Increased ad-spend. None of it worked.

Here's a dirty little secret that CEOs need to know. Unless the CEO is leading Starbucks or McDonalds or Target or a comparable brand, the CEO is going to have a hard time forcing customers to "be more loyal". Customers don't want to be "more loyal". How many widgets does a customer need?

Think about loyalty this way. If a customer shops Starbucks just one time a week, then the customer is purchasing 50 times a year. Assume that a loyalty program boosts purchases by 10%. At Starbucks, the loyalty program yields 50 * 0.10 = 5 additional purchases per year. Your typical e-commerce business possesses a customer who purchases maybe 2 or 3 times a year – 2.5 purchases per year is not uncommon (in fact, it is kind of high). A loyalty program that works just as well as a loyalty program at Starbucks yields 2.5 * 0.10 = 0.25 additional purchases per year. The new CEO is never going to see the impact of the program. The new CEO is far better off finding new customers.

I bring this up for a good reason! The new CEO, responsible for rebuilding the business, should rebuild the business around a sustainable strategy. Marketers are fired every-other-year for focusing on tactics and strategies that do not pay off. There's no need to attempt a rebuilding project around customer loyalty when the customer is not pre-disposed to become loyal. Why not rebuild around new customer acquisition programs?

Similarly, the new CEO should focus on new merchandise initiatives. I have worked on more than fifty merchandise forensics projects in the past three years. It is an all-too-common theme to speak with a CEO frustrated with the productivity of the merchandise assortment, only to learn that the merchandising team did not invest deep enough in new merchandise 2-3 years ago. The lack of investment results in too few winning items today. The CEO is looking for a quick fix, when the quick fix should have been implemented thirty months ago! If the CEO wants a successful rebuilding process, the CEO needs to encourage the merchandising team to immediately invest in new merchandise – today!!!

Look at what is called "class of" reporting. Analyze demand from new items by year – here is an old table from my merchandise forensics booklet.

Class Of	New Items	2011 Demand	2012 Demand	2013 Demand
2011 Items	383	$6,941,432	$7,412,444	$4,346,890
2012 Items	320	$0	$5,947,087	$4,977,865
2013 Items	291	$0	$0	$4,692,037
Total Demand		$25,989,908	$25,905,127	$22,814,491
% From New		27%	23%	21%

Notice that in this case, the business is losing volume, and demand from new items is on the decline (so are new items by year). Get this reporting as soon as you begin your rebuilding project, so that you know how to direct your merchandising team.

Develop a grading scheme for your merchandise assortment. Items in the top 5% for units and demand are "A", items in the top 5% for demand only are "B", items in the top 5% for units only are "C", items not A/B/C but in the top 45% for annual sales are "D", and all remaining items are "F". You want to see increases in A/B/C items over time – if you don't see increases in A/B/C items over time then the rebuild must immediately focus on new merchandise. Here is a table from my merchandise forensics booklet that illustrates what I am talking about.

	2013	2012	2011
A	32	35	38
B	31	34	33
C	31	36	49
D	465	534	497
F	683	634	637
Totals	1,242	1,273	1,254
A-C Tots.	94	105	120

This business has a significant decline in A/B/C items. There is a clear merchandising problem that must be addressed in this rebuilding project.

Expand the table to see how A/B/C items distribute across existing items and new items. It has been my experience that rebuilding projects must focus on new merchandise, simply because new merchandise development was ignored by the prior management regime.

Totals	2013	2012	2011
A	32	35	38
B	31	34	33
C	31	36	49
D	465	534	497
F	683	634	637
Totals	1,242	1,273	1,254
A-C Tots.	94	105	120

Existing	2013	2012	2011
A	27	28	29
B	25	29	26
C	24	27	36
D	353	379	332
F	522	491	449
Totals	951	954	872
A-C Tots.	76	84	91

New	2013	2012	2011
A	5	7	9
B	6	5	7
C	7	9	13
D	112	155	165
F	161	143	188
Totals	291	319	382
A-C Tots.	18	21	29

Look at the failure to develop new A/B/C items – from 29 in 2011 to 18 in 2013. Yes, existing item counts are in decline as well, but that frequently happens when new item development has been ignored for a long time.

Analyze how last year's items perform this year. The following table from my merchandise forensics book demonstrates that "D" and "F" items are unlikely to become winning A/B/C items.

2012 Grade	2012 Items	2013 Grade = A	2013 Grade = B	2013 Grade = C	2013 Grade = D	2013 Grade = F	2013 Not Avail.
A	35	20	2	4	4	3	2
B	34	1	17	0	12	2	2
C	36	0	0	14	18	3	1
D	534	4	2	5	277	170	76
F	634	2	4	1	42	344	241
New	291	5	6	7	112	161	0

When I observe a table like this, I recommend to Leadership to heavily invest in new merchandise.

It is popular to run five-year forecast models based on customer behavior. In any rebuilding project, I like to forecast the business based on merchandise evolution. If an item is a winning item (A/B/C), the item is expected to generate "$x" over the next "$y" years. Coupled with new merchandise development, we can forecast the trajectory of the business. The following table is also from my merchandise forensics booklet.

Merchandise Forensics Forecast

Items	Last Year	Today	After Year 1	After Year 2	After Year 3	After Year 4	After Year 5
Existing A	35	32	30	29	28	27	26
Existing B	34	31	29	27	27	26	25
Existing C	36	31	28	26	25	24	24
Existing D	534	462	423	400	385	376	370
Existing F	634	671	667	653	638	625	615
New A		5	5	5	5	5	5
New B		6	6	6	6	6	6
New C		7	7	7	7	7	7
New D		112	112	112	112	112	112
New F		161	161	161	161	161	161
Demand (in 000s)		$22,775	$21,155	$20,094	$19,368	$18,856	$18,492

If business is managed "as-is", the rebuilding effort will fail.

This is what the forecast looks like with an 80% increase in new merchandise.

Merchandise Forensics Forecast

Items	Last Year	Today	After Year 1	After Year 2	After Year 3	After Year 4	After Year 5
Existing A	35	32	34	36	38	39	41
Existing B	34	31	33	36	38	39	41
Existing C	36	31	33	35	36	37	38
Existing D	534	462	512	549	575	593	606
Existing F	634	671	796	879	934	972	999
New A		5	9	9	9	9	9
New B		6	11	11	11	11	11
New C		7	13	13	13	13	13
New D		112	202	202	202	202	202
New F		161	290	290	290	290	290
Demand (in 000s)		$22,775	$24,893	$26,552	$27,853	$28,846	$29,591

This is what a "rebuilt" business looks like! The new CEO understands that she must really ramp-up the product development process, if she wants to be successful.

We all read a ton of nonsense about "strategy". Lands' End had a strategy to transition to a fashion-centric business, torpedoing the core business in the process. A rebuilding project can align around multiple objectives. You can rebuild the core business while developing new business initiatives. You can run tables as illustrated above, and realize that the core business must be obliterated simply because there aren't ever going to be enough new items to fuel future success. You can purchase brands that align with your brand. There are many paths that yield a healthy rebuilding process. But make no mistake – the profit from the existing business will fund new endeavors – so it may not be wise to torpedo the core business in a gut-feel effort to grow.

But without the data, how could you possibly know whether you are headed down a reasonable rebuilding path?

Setting Objectives

The rebuilding process is dependent upon writing reasonable and achievable objectives.

Bonuses and objectives are essentially the same thing. In other words, I believe that any credible rebuilding project pays employees well for achieving objectives. Salary is not enough! Now, you are free to disagree with me, but I want every salaried employee to share in the success of the business.

All "Analyst" level employees should have a 15% bonus target.

All "Manager" level employees should have a 25% bonus target.

All "Director" level employees should have a 40% bonus target.

All "Vice President" level employees should have a 75% bonus target.

The "CEO" should have a 100% bonus target.

The bonus should be divided three ways.

I would assign 35% of the bonus to sales growth. I would assign 35% of the bonus to pre-tax profit rate. And I would assign 30% of the bonus to department-specific objectives. Sales growth and pre-tax profit improvement are common to every employee – every employee focuses on the same preferred outcome!

For instance, if the business is not generating sales growth and must achieve 10% sales growth to perform at a "playoff" level, then the objective might look like this.

Objective: Increase Annual Net Sales by 10%.

Exceeds Expectations (100% Payout) = 10%+ Sales Growth.
Meets Expectations (50% Payout) = 5% - 10% Sales Growth.
Missed Expectations (0% Payout) = < 5% Sales Growth.

The employee does not earn a bonus payout on this objective if sales growth is less than 5%. Progress must be made in order for the employee to earn a bonus.

Let's assume that the business is at 5% pre-tax profit and must get to 9% pre-tax profit for the business to get to "playoff" level performance.

Objective: Increase Pre-Tax Profit from 5% to 9%.

Exceeds Expectations (100% Payout) = Pre-Tax Profit > 9%.
Meets Expectations (50% Payout) = Pre-Tax Profit 7% to 9%.
Missed Expectations (0% Payout) = Pre-Tax Profit < 7%.

Finally, there should be an objective that is department-centric. In other words, there should be a merchandising objective for the merchandising team, a marketing objective for the marketing team, and an operations-centric objective for the operations team.

Recall our earlier example where new merchandise success had to be 80% better than it currently is? This is what the objective might look like for the merchandising team.

Objective: Increase Winning New Items from 18 To 33 Per Year.

Exceeds Expectations (100% Payout) = 33 or More New Winning Items.
Meets Expectations (50% Payout) = 25 to 32 New Winning Items.
Missed Expectations (0% Payout) = Fewer Than 25 New Winning Items.

Assume that the marketing team must increase the number of new + reactivated customers by 20% to grow the business at a sufficient rate. Here is the marketing objective.

Objective: Increase New + Reactivated Buyer Growth by 20%.

Exceeds Expectations (100% Payout) = > 20% Increase.
Meets Expectations (50% Payout) = 10% - 20% Increase.

Missed Expectations (0% Payout) = < 10% Increase.

Alright – let's pretend that we have a Marketing Analyst earning $60,000 per year. The employee is eligible for a maximum bonus of 15% * $60,000 = $9,000. Let's pretend that Net Sales grew by 6%, let's pretend that pre-tax profit was 6%, and let's pretend that new + reactivated buyers grew by 25%.

Net Sales = $9,000 * 35% of Bonus Objective * 50% of Payout.

Pre-Tax Profit = $9,000 * 35% of Objective * 0% of Payout.

New/Reactivated = $9,000 * 30% of Objective * 100% of Payout.

Bonus Payout = $1,575 + $0 + $2,700 = $4,275.

The Chief Marketing Officer earns $200,000 per year, and is eligible for a 75% payout of $150,000. The math is similar, but the base is much higher.

Net Sales = $150,000 * 35% of Bonus Objective * 50% of Payout.

Pre-Tax Profit = $150,000 * 35% of Objective * 0% of Payout.

New/Reactivated = $150,000 * 30% of Objective * 100% of Payout.

Bonus Payout = $26,250 + $0 + $45,000 = $71,250.

Every employee can easily identify the metrics that yield a healthy bonus payout. The metrics align with metrics that demonstrate that the business has been "rebuilt".

I know, I know, you don't like the idea of Analyst / Manager level employees earning bonuses. You think these folks are pawns on a chessboard that you move around for your own benefit. That's lizard logic!

If you are a $100,000,000 business and have 100 Analyst/Manager level employees, then the most successful year you can have likely results in an average of $15,000 in bonus payments across each of 100 staffers, or $1,500,000. That's the maximum – likely payments are half of that total. So you are likely paying 1% of net sales on bonus payments to Analyst/Manager staff. You can cut that out of your advertising budget and never miss it! In fact, hire a vendor to do just that for you – and reallocate the money to your existing Analysts/Managers.

Do you think your staff will work harder on your initiatives if you are paying them bonuses to work on your rebuilding project?

Now that you have your bonus / objective structure solidified, make sure to report on your performance. Private information that cannot be publicly published is shared every week – pre-tax profit and sales projections, new customer counts, new merchandise success, that kind of thing. Constantly communicate, constantly remind your team how the company is progressing on this rebuilding project.

Use flat-screen televisions in key conference rooms to publish "Top-10" lists … the stuff that is selling well that day. Publish a list of Existing Items, New Items, Top-10 by Product Category, Top-10 by Region, Top-10 by Price Point, Top-10 by Marketing Channel, Top-10 by Store, Top-10 Performing Stores. Teach every employee how merchandise performs, especially your marketing team. In order for a rebuilding project to succeed, marketers must know the merchandise that is selling best, and must know how to personalize the merchandise assortment to individual customers.

FYI – a percentage of your employee base DO NOT WANT TO REBUILD! They want to do things the way they've always been done. I can speak from personal experience. In my final months at Nordstrom, I was given a new boss. This individual wanted to rebuild my area according to her vision – you certainly can't blame her for wanting to do that, right? A couple of times a week, she'd ask me "*are you onboarding?*" In her first month on the job, she'd ask me to help "*onboard*" my employees to her plan. Well … I didn't want to have anything to do with her plan … it was *her* plan, not *my* plan. Let's just say that I wasn't a "willing spirit". I knew it was time to leave the company. But too often, the individual does not want to leave the company, and does not want to go through a rebuilding process. That person could poison your rebuilding program.

I took over a team in 2002. I can recall walking into a conference room, and hearing one of my employees tell another employee *"all we have to do is wait him out, he'll be gone in a year or two like everybody who came before him."*

As CEO, you may have hundreds of employees who feel this way. Many of your direct reports may feel this way – many may have been passed over for your position! At the very start of the rebuilding process, make it clear that if employees do not want to go through this journey with you, they should walk out the front door and find a new job. And when you learn that your team is not on your side, act swiftly – ask the employee to join the rebuilding process immediately, or remove the employee from the company and offer a more-than-fair severance package as a lovely parting gift.

Let's talk about an additional aspect of objective setting. The table below shows the fifteen-year trajectory of Gap (Gap reports Operating Income, which is modestly greater than EBT, thereby modestly overstating won/lost records by maybe a quarter of a win).

Year	Net Sales	Pre-Tax %	NS Incr	Wins	Losses
2001	$13,847,873	1.7%			
2002	$14,454,709	5.5%	4.4%	8	8
2003	$15,854,000	12.0%	9.7%	11	5
2004	$16,267,000	12.8%	2.6%	10	6
2005	$16,023,000	10.9%	-1.5%	9	7
2006	$15,923,000	7.7%	-0.6%	8	8
2007	$15,763,000	8.3%	-1.0%	8	8
2008	$14,526,000	10.7%	-7.8%	8	8
2009	$14,197,000	12.8%	-2.3%	10	6
2010	$14,664,000	13.4%	3.3%	11	5
2011	$14,549,000	9.9%	-0.8%	9	7
2012	$15,651,000	12.4%	7.6%	11	5
2013	$16,148,000	13.3%	3.2%	11	5
2014	$16,435,000	12.7%	1.8%	10	6
2015	$15,797,000	9.6%	-3.9%	8	8

As you know, Gap made a CEO change at the start of 2015 – the won/lost record indicates that the business is trending negatively. And historically, Gap has generated average to above-average performance, largely due to their ability to generate profit. Sales have been stuck for twelve years, and if we account for inflation, it's a likely 20% inflation-adjusted sales drop.

When you consider that e-commerce accounts for about 16% of total Gap sales (vs. a percentage or two back in 2003), there is a channel alignment issue that must be reconciled in the rebuilding process. Between inflationary changes and e-commerce channel switching, retail stores may have lost 30% of their potential volume over the past thirteen years.

Be very careful in calibrating bonus structure for businesses going through channel shift. It may not be possible to grow Gap in-store sales at high rates (especially in the short-term). It may be easy to grow Gap e-commerce sales, especially in the short term (in fact, it usually is easy – spend more ad dollars). Where possible, align incentives with total business performance. I have observed too many cases where average e-commerce employees are greatly rewarded while talented retail employee are penalized – all because the customer is shifting behavior away from stores. I have plenty of catalog-centric clients – some of their employees were penalized because catalogs drove sales to the e-commerce channel. When rebuilding a company, one wants to rebuild the whole company, and not reward a fraction of employees for performance that they may not have earned.

Encouragement

Rebuilding should be fun! It isn't terribly hard to maintain a successful business. It is very hard to turn around a floundering business, but the fruits of the turnaround effort are very sweet!

I have learned that some employees respond to sales gains/losses – especially merchandising teams. Those employees tend to be easier to motivate than others. I have learned that almost no employees care about profit. I've always wondered why that is the case? Today, I believe that employees don't care about profit because they don't share in profit. Public companies return profit to shareholders. Private companies return profit to the owner. Startups are generally unprofitable, and if startups grow at a fast rate, employees are rewarded with stock. In other words, there are very few cases where non-financial employees need to care about profit.

And yet, profit is the namesake of the "profit and loss" statement. It's a terribly important metric.

That's why I convert sales increases and pre-tax profit rates into NFL-style "Wins and Losses". It's hard to tell if a 3% sales decline and a 3% pre-tax profit is good/bad *"but we are still profitable, right?"* It's easy to look at a won/lost record and say, *"wow, 5-11 is terrible, we are losing."*

The framework gives us an opportunity to measure different ideas. Here is a high-level table of wins by sales gain and pre-tax profit.

Annual Wins

Sales Change	Annual Pre-Tax Profit									
	-20.0%	-16.0%	-12.0%	-8.0%	-4.0%	0.0%	4.0%	8.0%	12.0%	16.0%
50.0%	4	5	7	9	10	12	13	14	15	15
45.0%	3	5	6	8	10	11	13	14	14	15
40.0%	3	4	5	7	9	11	12	13	14	15
35.0%	2	3	5	6	8	10	11	13	14	14
30.0%	2	3	4	6	7	9	11	12	13	14
25.0%	2	3	4	5	7	8	10	12	13	14
20.0%	1	2	3	4	6	8	9	11	12	13
15.0%	1	2	3	4	5	7	9	10	12	13
10.0%	1	2	2	3	5	6	8	10	11	12
5.0%	1	1	2	3	4	5	7	9	10	12
0.0%	1	1	2	2	3	5	6	8	10	11
-5.0%	1	1	1	2	3	4	6	7	9	11
-10.0%	0	1	1	2	2	4	5	6	8	10
-15.0%	0	1	1	1	2	3	4	6	7	9
-20.0%	0	1	1	1	2	3	4	5	7	8

Let's assume you lead a $100,000,000 brand that generates 4% pre-tax profit. Your business is not growing. You essentially lead a business that is posting a 6-10 style NFL record – not good, not good at all. Let's assume that your merchandising team finds a way to grow the business by 5%. If profit remains flat (it won't, profit will grow), you are now managing a business with a 7-9 style NFL record. The efforts of your merchandising team are essentially worth one NFL win. Hint – it's hard to account for an incremental win in the NFL!! And if pre-tax profit grows to 6%, your business now has an 8-8 NFL record. If your marketing team finds a way to cut two points out of the ad-to-sales ratio, well, you might just have a business that has a 9-7 NFL record. You went from a losing business to a business that is nearly at "playoff quality" with just a few changes.

In other words, employees learn how small changes transform a losing brand into a winning brand. By transforming the profit and loss statement, we motivate employees to make changes that facilitate the rebuilding process.

Look, it is hard enough to turn around a losing brand. The CEO faces too many challenges, too much outside interference, and has too few advocates on her side. Why not leverage the tools at your disposal?

Use the won/lost concept to illustrate where you are in your rebuilding journey.

Use the won/lost concept to illustrate how your competition is performing. Create a dashboard that lists the "standings" – your record vs. each publicly traded competitor.

Early in your tenure, determine if your business model "retains" customers or not. Most of my clients operate a business model where low-cost customer acquisition is the most important factor in business success.

Early in your tenure, determine if your merchandise assortment is helping or hurting rebuilding efforts. 80% of my client base have merchandising problems that stem from not harvesting enough winning new items. These problems appear 2-3 years after they were born, so the problem must be diagnosed early if you want your rebuilding effort to succeed.

Make sure every salaried employee is bonus eligible. Every one. This might cost you 1% of net sales – find expenses to trim elsewhere. If you are going to make investments, prioritize investment in your employees over those who work for the vendors who support you.

Divide your bonus objectives according to what is important to your business. Thirty-five percent of bonus potential should be paid if sales gains exceed expectations. Thirty-five percent of bonus potential should be paid if pre-tax profit rates exceed expectations. Thirty percent of bonus potential should be paid if department-specific goals (new customer counts, new merchandise success, website conversion rate improvements, operational cost reductions) are exceeded.

Avoid pitting divisions or channels against each other, especially in retail where e-commerce is cannibalizing the retail channel.

Treat your staff well.

Have fun rebuilding a business!

www.ingramcontent.com/pod-product-compliance
Lightning Source LLC
Chambersburg PA
CBHW040859180526
45159CB00001B/469